D1375341

Schools

Richard Northcott

Contents

OXFORD
UNIVERSITY PRESS

UNIVERSITY PRESS

Great Clarendon Street, Oxford, OX2 6DP, United Kingdom

Oxford University Press is a department of the University
of Oxford. It furthers the University's objective of excellence in
research, scholarship, and education by publishing worldwide.
Oxford is a registered trade mark of Oxford University Press
in the UK and in certain other countries

ISBN: 978 0 19 464627 7

An Audio CD Pack containing this book and a CD is also
available, ISBN 978 0 19 464637 6

The CD has a choice of American and British English
recordings of the complete text.

An accompanying Activity Book is also available,
ISBN 978 0 19 464648 2

Printed in China

This book is printed on paper from certified and
well-managed sources.

ACKNOWLEDGEMENTS

Illustrations by: Kelly Kennedy p.10; Alan Rowe pp.20, 21, 22,
23, 24, 25, 26, 27, 29, 30, 31.

*The Publishers would also like to thank the following for their
kind permission to reproduce photographs and other copyright
material:* Alamy pp.3 (Interfoto/Travel/big school Oman),
5 (Louise Murray/sledge, Simon Rawles/bike), 6 (Bill
Bachman), 7 (Nathan Benn/big school Korea), 8 (Heiner
Heine/imagebroker), 10 (Keith Dannemiller), 11 (Martin
Shields/science class), 13 (Yaacov Shein/boat canteen),
14 (Maggiegowan.co.uk), 15 (Jean Schweitzer/Peru school),
16 (Ton Koene/Picture Contact BV), 17 (Andrew Woodley/
school garden); Corbis pp.3 (David Bathgate/boat school),
9 (Matthias Tunger/students outside class), 11 (Anders Ryman/
PE class), 15 (Roger Ressmeyer/hard hat students), 19(Louie
Psihoyos); Getty Images pp.7 (Bruno Morandi/Reportage/
open air school Nepal), 9 (Cancan Chu/Getty Images News/
cave school), 12 (Yellow Dog Productions/The Image Bank),
13 (Yellow Dog Productions/The Image Bank/children eating);
Lonely Planet Images p.17 (Keren Su/school band); Oxford
University Press p.18; Rex Features p.4 (Design Pics Inc).

 # Introduction

There are schools all around the world. There are big schools and little schools, new schools and old schools.

Is your school big or little?
Is your school new or old?

 Now read and discover more about schools!

Let's Go to School

All around the world, students go to school. Some students walk to school, and some go by bus or by train. Some students go by bicycle, and some go by car.

These students are in the USA. They go to school by bus.

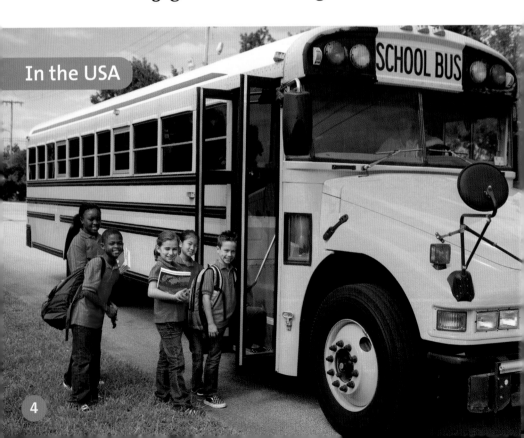

In the USA

In Canada

sled

In the snow in Canada, some students go to school by sled. In India, some students go to school by rickshaw. How do you go to school?

In India

rickshaw

Go to page 20 for activities.

2 Buildings

In Australia

Let's look at school buildings around the world. This school is in Australia. It's in the countryside. It's a little school, but many schools in Australia are big.

Here's a big school in a city. Many students go to this school. It has a big school playground. This school is in South Korea.

Discover!

For these students in Nepal, the countryside is their school!

Go to page 21 for activities.

3 At School

These students are at school. They meet their friends. They talk and they are happy.

Listen! That's the bell. Let's go to the classroom.

A Teacher and Her Students

The students stand in the hallway by the door. The teacher says, 'Hello, everyone.' These students have books and notebooks. Can you see them? No, you can't. They are in their bags.

Discover!

One school in China is in a cave!

Go to page 22 for activities.

An English Class

In the classroom, the teacher says, 'Sit down, please. Open your English books.' It's an English class.

The teacher has a picture. She says, 'What's this?' One student says, 'It's a giraffe.'

Put up your hand when you want to speak in class.

A Science Class

In some classes, students have computers. Do you have computers in your classroom?

In physical education classes, students run, jump, and play. These girls play basketball in their physical education classes.

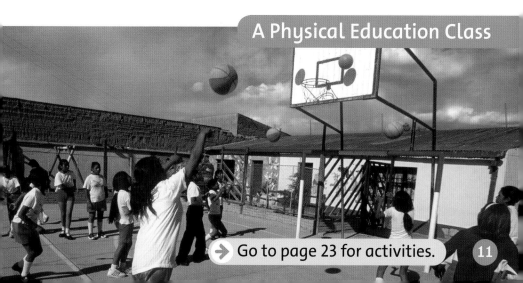

A Physical Education Class

Go to page 23 for activities.

5 Lunchtime

lunch lady

At lunchtime, these students go to the cafeteria. The lunch lady gives them food. She puts their food on a plate. The students put their plate on a tray and say, 'Thank you.'

The students sit down and eat. They talk to their friends. 'How are you?' … 'What's your favorite soccer team?' … 'Do you have a computer?'

Discover!

One school in Cambodia is a boat. The cafeteria is a boat, too!

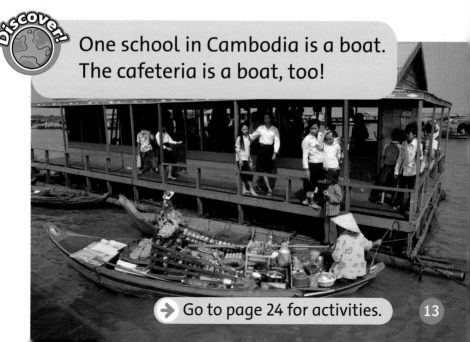

Go to page 24 for activities.

6 Uniform

In China

These students in China wear a uniform. The girls wear red pants and the boys wear black pants. Everyone wears a white shirt and a red tie. Students don't wear a uniform in every school in China.

In Peru

These students in Peru wear a uniform, too. Everyone wears a purple sweater and a white shirt. The girls wear a gray skirt and the boys wear gray pants. Students don't wear a uniform in every school in Peru.

Do you wear a uniform?

hard hat

These students in Japan wear a hard hat. Their school is near a volcano.

→ Go to page 25 for activities.

Free Time

Students have free time in the day. They run in the school playground or they talk to their friends. Some students play soccer or basketball. These boys and girls play soccer in their free time.

Students have free time after school, too. In some schools, there's a garden. There are flowers and vegetables in the garden. Students help in the garden after school.

In some schools, there's a band. Students play in the band after school.

A School Garden

A School Band

Go to page 26 for activities.

 8 School Trips

Students like school trips. On these days, students don't go to school. They go with their teacher to a zoo or a museum.

The zoo is a favorite school trip for many students. They can see animals and learn about them. These students can see an otter.

At a Zoo

otter

dinosaur skeleton

At a Museum

Museums are a good school trip, too. These students are in a great museum. The museum has a dinosaur skeleton!

Students go on great school trips and they learn many new things. They learn many new things with their teachers at school, too.

Thank you, teachers!

→ Go to page 27 for activities.

1 Let's Go to School

← Read pages 4–5.

1 Find and write the words.

d	b	u	s	q	i	a
w	o	r	s	l	e	d
v	a	q	c	o	t	r
d	t	z	p	h	e	j
b	t	r	a	i	n	v
o	m	k	c	a	r	n
s	t	b	w	o	a	q
b	i	c	y	c	l	e

1 _bus_

2 _s_

3 _t_

4 _b_

5 _c_

2 Complete the sentences.

bus   school   ~~students~~   walk

1 All around the world, _students_ go to school.

2 Some students _____ to school.

3 Some students go by _____.

4 How do you go to _____?

② Buildings

← Read pages 6–7.

1 Write *true* or *false*.

1 Many schools in Australia are big.   _true_

2 Students in South Korea don't
go to school.   _____

3 Some schools have a school
playground.   _____

4 Some schools don't have buildings.   _____

2 Write the words.

| city   countryside   playground   ~~school~~ |

1 ___school___

2 _____

3 _____

4 _____

3 At School

← Read pages 8–9.

1 Write the words. Then match.

1 lble

_____bell_____

2 gab

_____

3 lsrocsmao

_____

4 laywlah

_____

2 Circle the correct words.

1 The students stand in the **friends** / **hallway**.

2 The teacher **says** / **stands**, 'Hello, everyone.'

3 The students have **books** / **hallways**.

4 The books are in their **door** / **bags**.

4 In Class

← Read pages 10–11.

1 Complete the sentences.

> books   classes   have   teacher

1 The _____ says, 'Sit down, please.'

2 The teacher says, 'Open your _____.'

3 In some classes, students _____ computers.

4 In physical education _____, students run, jump, and play.

2 Write the words.

> book   basketball   computer   picture

1 _____   3 _____

2 _____   4 _____

⑤ Lunchtime

← Read pages 12–13.

1 Find and write the words.

r	f	o	o	d	g	i	t
l	v	e	p	l	a	t	e
t	h	t	c	j	e	r	o
r	x	z	o	t	f	o	o
p	r	t	r	a	y	k	s
i	p	s	y	s	a	l	e
b	o	a	t	a	y	n	o

1 b _____   2 f _____

3 p _____   4 t _____

2 Complete the sentences.

you   plate   food   cafeteria

1 At lunchtime, some students go to the

_____.

2 A lunch lady gives them _____.

3 She puts their food on a _____.

4 The students say, 'Thank _____.'

(6) Uniform

← Read pages 14–15.

1 Write *true* or *false*.

1 Some students in China wear a uniform. _____

2 Students wear a uniform in every school in China. _____

3 Some girls in Peru wear a gray skirt at school. _____

4 Students don't wear a uniform in Japan. _____

2 Write the words.

sweater   shirt   tie   skirt

1 _____   3 _____

2 _____   4 _____

7 Free Time

← Read pages 16–17.

1 Write the words. Then match.

1 dbna

_____

2 sccreo

_____

3 elagveetbs

_____

4 lworefs

_____

2 Circle the correct words.

1 Students have **free time** / **playground** in the day.

2 Some students talk to their **soccer** / **friends**.

3 Some students help in the garden after **school** / **flowers**.

4 Some students **run** / **play** in a band.

8 School Trips

← Read pages 18–19.

1 Complete the sentences.

animals   dinosaur   learn   trips   zoo

1 Students like school _____ .

2 The _____ is a favorite school trip.

3 Students can see _____ at the zoo.

4 Some museums have _____ skeletons.

5 Students _____ many new things on school trips.

2 Complete the puzzle.

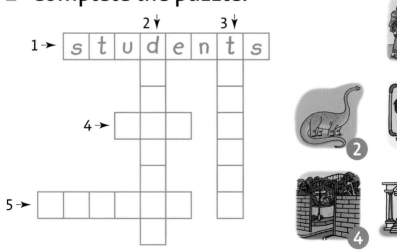

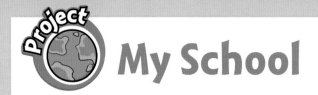

My School

1 Find or draw a picture of your school.

2 Write about your school.

What is the name of your school?

The name is _____

Where is it?

_____

How do you go to school?

_____

What class are you in?

_____

How many students are in your class?

_____

What is the name of your teacher?

_____

3 **Draw and color a new uniform for your school. Write about your uniform.**

a white shirt

The boys wear a white shirt,

_____

_____

The girls wear

_____

_____

Picture Dictionary

 animals

 band

 basketball

 bell

 boat

 buildings

 bus

 cafeteria

 cave

 city

 classroom

 countryside

 food

 hallway

 near

 pants

picture   plate   playground   school

shirt   skirt   soccer team   speak

students   sweater   teacher   tie

tray   vegetables   volcano   world

Oxford Read and Discover

Series Editor: Hazel Geatches • CLIL Adviser: John Clegg

Oxford Read and Discover graded readers are at six levels, for students from age 6 and older. They cover many topics within three subject areas, and support English across the curriculum, or Content and Language Integrated Learning (CLIL).

Available for each reader:
• Audio Pack
• Activity Book

Available for selected readers:
• e-Books

Teaching notes & CLIL guidance: **www.oup.com/elt/teacher/readanddiscover**

Subject Area / Level	The World of Science & Technology	The Natural World	The World of Arts & Social Studies
1 — 300 headwords	• Eyes • Fruit • Trees • Wheels	• At the Beach • In the Sky • Wild Cats • Young Animals	• Art • Schools
2 — 450 headwords	• Electricity • Plastic • Sunny and Rainy • Your Body	• Camouflage • Earth • Farms • In the Mountains	• Cities • Jobs
3 — 600 headwords	• How We Make Products • Sound and Music • Super Structures • Your Five Senses	• Amazing Minibeasts • Animals in the Air • Life in Rainforests • Wonderful Water	• Festivals Around the World • Free Time Around the World
4 — 750 headwords	• All About Plants • How to Stay Healthy • Machines Then and Now • Why We Recycle	• All About Desert Life • All About Ocean Life • Animals at Night • Incredible Earth	• Animals in Art • Wonders of the Past
5 — 900 headwords	• Materials to Products • Medicine Then and Now • Transportation Then and Now • Wild Weather	• All About Islands • Animal Life Cycles • Exploring Our World • Great Migrations	• Homes Around the World • Our World in Art
6 — 1,050 headwords	• Cells and Microbes • Clothes Then and Now • Incredible Energy • Your Amazing Body	• All About Space • Caring for Our Planet • Earth Then and Now • Wonderful Ecosystems	• Food Around the World • Helping Around the World